WRITING FOR
THE BAR EXAM

Andrew P. Connors, Esq.
Cherie Washburn, Esq.

This book is best used along with the personalized services of Esquire Education. Please visit our website at http://esqeducation.com for further details.

Not all products and services mentioned in this book are the trademarks or service marks of Esquire Education. Kaplan PMBR, BarBri, and other marks are the property of their respective owners and are used only in an editorial fashion, with no intention of infringement. Use of a product or service name or term in this publication should not be construed as affecting the validity of any trademark or service mark.

Printed in the United States of America.

Published under license by Esquire Education.

"[T]he genius is having a ten-dollar idea in a five-cent sentence, not having a five-cent idea in a ten-dollar sentence."

- Justice Clarence Thomas[1]

---

[1] Bryan A. Garner, *Interviews with United States Supreme Court Justices*, 13 SCRIBES J. OF LEGAL WRITING 100 (2010).

Acknowledgements

The authors would like to thank several people for making this book and their careers as lawyers possible. We would like to thank our spouses, Allison and Craig, who have supported us both financially and emotionally. We would also like to thank all of those that played a part in helping us make this book a reality, especially Dave Gilbert and Ben Walton. Finally, and above all else, we thank God, who loves us despite our sins, provides us with our ideas and inspiration, and sustains us in the good times and the bad. Thank you.

Contents

Introduction

Why Use This Book?

Traditional bar review programs like BarBri or Kaplan PMBR are a necessary resource for anyone taking a state bar exam. However, those programs are incomplete. Those programs provide you with a good review of the key subjects found on the bar exam, but they do not teach you how to write a good essay. That is where this book comes in.

This book provides you with a focused series of lessons and examples, along with a comprehensive methodology, that will ensure that your essay writing is as clear, concise, and effective as it can be. Certainly, the traditional programs provide you with the structure you need to stay focused and to use your relatively limited time effectively. They will also require you to write a fair number of practice essays in preparation for the essay portions that every state bar exam contains. You should sign up for one of the traditional programs to ensure your bar success; this book merely complements those programs. The traditional programs do not provide in-depth instruction on the *mechanics* of constructing a good essay. They do not show you how to organize and persuasively apply facts, to assess the problem, or to write efficiently, persuasively, and effectively. *This book does.*

Why We Wrote This Book

When we prepared for the Virginia bar exam in the summer of 2010, we were generally satisfied with the comprehensive review of the various legal areas provided by our respective programs. However, we were also generally disappointed with the guidance provided on essay writing. Since essay writing made up 60% of our score in Virginia,[2] we found the gaps we saw in our respective programs quite perturbing. Both of our programs required us to practice essays, but each often left us with puzzling, incomplete answers to compare with our work. The answers

---

[2] Indeed, in most or all U.S. jurisdictions, the essay portion of the bar exam makes up a substantial part of your score.

generally had the right idea in terms of substance, but they usually did not have a *full* essay written as you would expect to see it written on the bar exam. The sample answers generally felt like they were missing something. Oftentimes, they did not use good syntax or have a good organizational structure, and they rarely assessed issues in a complete manner. The feedback from our program-assigned "mentors" was no better. Our mentors always gave us a "grade," but never told us what our answer needed to get us over the hump. They never told us how to write a truly complete answer to a bar exam essay.

After taking the exam, we considered these issues more fully. Although practically no one would labor under the false idea that the sample answers provided by these programs generally represent well-written answers, not everyone preparing for the exam would adequately understand what good bar exam writing actually looked like. To prepare for the bar exam, we would have liked to have known *precisely* what a good exam answer looked like, and thus, whether our practice answers, if written on the actual exam, would get the maximum points possible. Did we understand what the question was asking us—the underlying issue the question was *really* getting at? Did we accurately and appropriately identify the issue? Did we correctly assess the facts and appropriately construct our rule discussion in light of the particular facts and the issue presented? Did we appropriately apply the facts to the law, using good grammar, syntax, and persuasive writing to convey why our assessment was right and why the facts should not lead us in another direction? Did we effectively state a conclusion that appropriately answered the question? These are the sorts of questions a bar exam essay writer needs to consider, but this fact was not necessarily conveyed by the traditional bar preparation courses we utilized.

Good Writing Just Might Make a Difference

We came to find that many other people had the same concerns that we had about writing a complete answer. We also realized that, for some people, those concerns also translated into deficiencies in essay writing that probably affected their performance on the bar exam. This included Cherie Washburn, one of the co-authors of this book. She recognized that she had gaps in her essay writing. Due in part to those gaps, she had to face the hard reality of failing the bar exam on her first attempt in the summer of 2010. Here are her thoughts on what she went through when she found out that she had not passed the bar:

> When I was studying for the bar, I started out as almost every other graduating law student starts, with a comprehensive bar study course. I attended every class, took good notes, made flash cards and memorized as much as my brain could handle. I felt like I was on the same track as everyone else and that my efforts would enable me to pass the exam. I assumed that I would make the bar pass rate cut-off of 75% passage in Virginia, especially because I was slightly above average in my law school class. Surely, I would not be in the bottom 25% of bar takers!

> I felt nervous going into the exam, but I also felt like I had studied enough to pass. I had so much substantive material memorized that I thought no matter what was on the exam I would be able to put the correct legal rule down. I thought that was the most important thing—to know the rule and state the rule. If I could do that, I would get a passing grade. Every professor, bar study teacher, and former law school student whom I had spoken with all said the same thing: just know the rule and you will be fine.

> I am here to tell you that knowing the rules and memorizing the acronyms will not be enough and you will not be fine. There is a key ingredient missing: properly identifying the facts that trigger the issues you should be talking about and writing an effective answer. Your

answer must be complete and thorough. It must include accurate, precise analysis. If your answer just regurgitates facts and sprinkles in some memorized rules, your score will fall short.

I did not pass the bar exam when I took it for the first time in the summer of 2010. It is difficult to describe the feeling you get when your name is not on the list. You think there must be some mistake—this can't be happening! It is an awful feeling that stays for months after the initial shock, and it is a feeling I would not wish on any future bar exam taker. That is why I think this book is so important. I did not understand how to write an essay properly. I knew the rules, I put in the study time, and I practiced, but that was not enough. I did not understand how to write a bar exam essay effectively.

The Bar Exam is a Hard Test

Cherie's results were disappointing, but they did not speak to her ability as a lawyer. Her friends, colleagues, and professors knew that she could pass. The bar exam will sometimes get the best of people that have the ability and skill to make fantastic lawyers. It is a hard test—probably the hardest test you will ever take. You will spend many sleepless nights trying to cram all the minutiae the examiners might conceivably ask you into your head. At the end of a long road of studying, you will find yourself tired and disheveled. We had the same experiences ourselves. *Be prepared.*

Improved Writing Actually Made a Difference

Despite rigorous study, you could still find yourself just barely below a passing score when you receive the results of the exam months after taking it. We hope that this book will ensure that you are not one of the many attorneys-to-be that finds themselves a few points away from a passing score, a coveted license to practice law just barely out of your reach. This book is the product of months of exploration and study by the co-authors of this book. We carefully considered how to write well on the bar exam. With lots of practice, we collectively improved average answers to exceptional answers. We think it had something to do with the passing score Cherie Washburn received on her subsequent attempt on the Virginia Bar Exam in the spring of 2011. As she tells it:

> I remember when I finally understood how to write a proper bar exam essay during a study session. I thought to myself, "This is not impossible; in fact, it's a formula—and I get it!" When I sat for the bar exam in February of 2011, I was, of course, anxious, as anyone would be in my shoes. Yet, when I turned over the exam and I saw that this was just another question like the hundreds I had done before, I knew I could do it. I did not panic. I stayed focused on what I knew, and I wrote my essays in an organized format. By the end of the first day, I knew I had performed well on the essay portion. By doing that, the MBE day became less stressful.

> On the day the results came out, I just could not bear to look at the list notifying the world of those that passed the exam. When a friend finally called me in the afternoon to let me know that I had passed, I felt a huge weight lift off my shoulders. I was so excited; I was speechless. It is truly a moment in your life when you look at yourself and think, "I am a proud, successful attorney and my career is about to begin!" I hope the approach described in this book will do for you what it did for me.

Our Hope for You

It is our hope that the methodology provided in this book will help you to have the same good results that it had for us. This book presents a systematic method for you to follow when you answer bar exam essays. It also includes examples for you as we teach the concepts that will improve your bar exam essay writing. For some of you, this improvement will be significant. For others, it may be less so. In many cases, however, even slight improvement may make the difference in passing the bar. We hope it makes that difference for you.

The Contents of This Book

The first chapter of this book reviews the basics of good legal writing. The second chapter describes the first step of our systematic process: assessing the question. The third chapter confronts the second step: fully describing the rule of law. The fourth chapter completes our systematic approach by fully explaining how to apply the rule to the facts in a rigorous manner.

Our book does not describe a simple "IRAC" method, although it certainly conforms in many respects to that well-known organizational method. Our method differs in emphasis—an emphasis that many people never grasped in law school. Our method does not call on you to recount rules and list facts in a bland, haphazard manner. Instead, it establishes a systematic method for intelligently identifying the issue presented, for developing a rule statement adapted with the question in mind, and for persuasively showing how the facts result in the conclusion that makes up your answer to the question. It uses examples throughout and requires you to do some exercises, which culminate in a comprehensive methodology you can apply to your own practice questions and those that we provide in this book.

The examples in this book, and their accompanying answers, are demarcated by a gray box. For all the examples in this book, we also include comprehensive model answers on the particular aspects those questions are meant to teach. You will also find additional practice questions and answers in Chapter 5. In Chapter 6, we conclude with some final thoughts on the journey ahead of you, and some reminders for exam day.

How to Use This Book

You should read this book and work through the examples provided before you begin your comprehensive bar review course. The earlier you begin the better. This will allow you the time you need to assess your skill level, to improve that skill level on your own, and to obtain further help if necessary.

When you do the examples in this book, we want you to assess where you are at with both your writing skill and the substantive law. To do that, start every problem in this book without study aids or other outside materials. If you have difficulty recalling the law, then you should review outside materials, but then close those materials when actually writing your answer. For the problems found in Chapters 1 through 4, take as much time as you need. For Chapter 5, we would like you to start timing yourself. We provide specific times for each of the questions in that Chapter. By timing yourself, you will start to get a better idea of your skill level before you start your comprehensive review course.

Finally, we should note that, in most cases, we have used general common law rules in this book when answering questions, or applicable federal law. The purpose of doing this is to get you thinking again about subjects you may have learned long ago, not to teach you the law in any comprehensive manner. This is especially true in light of the fact that the United States has many jurisdictions, and the rules in your jurisdiction may vary from the rules presented in this book. The rules provided here are merely first steps; you should rely on your comprehensive program to learn the definitive rules applicable in your jurisdiction. Indeed, on a couple of occasions, we have included minor questions relating to Virginia court procedure. We do this primarily because it is common for essay questions to mix in some basic court procedure into questions about more substantive law. Thus, when you come to these instances in our examples, but you do not intend to practice in Virginia, we suggest you take the time to research the procedure applicable in your jurisdiction and to answer the question as if it were directed at your jurisdiction.

Final Thoughts

You will come to find in the months of study ahead that the support of friends and family will play an instrumental part in your success (and sanity.) Be sure to take the time to thank those people for their support, including those that have brought you this far. In that light, we must conclude this introduction by again thanking all of those that made this book and our law careers possible. To our wonderful spouses, Allison and Craig—we could not have come this far without your support. To our professors, thank you for teaching us. To our fellow classmates, thank you for sharing in all the sleepless nights. Most especially, we thank God, whose strength and inspiration has continually blessed us. We pray that He will bless you on your long journey ahead.

Should you find yourself wanting more direction and advice, please visit our website at http://esqeducation.com. There you will find more articles on legal writing and related subjects. You can also learn more about the various services we offer that can improve your writing even further.

Chapter 1:
Legal Writing Basics

Introduction

Before we get into our systematic approach to bar exam essay writing, we would first like to review some basics of good legal writing. This review does not cover good writing *generally*; as someone who has now completed at least seven years of higher education, you should have a reasonably good grasp on the English language. Nevertheless, we recognize that legal writing is a difficult skill that not everyone will expertly grasp. Here, we focus on some critical tips and techniques for good legal writing, and demonstrate them with examples and exercises for reinforcement.

Avoid Passive Voice

We have to start with this one first. You should mostly avoid writing in passive voice. Of course, one—if not several—of your law school professors probably told you this. Nevertheless, you might still frequently employ passive voice in your writing; that is normal—many law students and even many lawyers tend to fall into this habit. In fact, this intractable problem might come in part from the fact that many people have a hard time understanding what, exactly, writing in passive voice entails.

A sentence written in passive voice makes the subject of the sentence the thing acted upon rather than the thing performing the action. A sentence in passive voice generally contains a form of the verb "to be." Oftentimes, a sentence written in passive voice will not mention the thing doing the action. In those cases, you will need to add the thing doing the action to change the sentence to active voice.

Passive Voice Example

> **Passive Voice:** The decision was made that a police officer must stop interrogating a suspect when he asks for a lawyer.

Active Voice: The Court held that a police officer must stop interrogating a suspect when he asks for a lawyer.

If a passive sentence includes all of the necessary nouns, you should re-arrange the sentence so that the subject is performing the action, and thereby eliminate the form of the verb "to be" in the sentence.

Another Passive Voice Example

Passive Voice: The argument was not made by the attorney in the trial court below.

Active Voice: The attorney did not make the argument in the trial court below.

Now try your hand at writing the following sentences in active voice. You will find model answers to this exercise on the following page.

Passive Voice Exercise

1. The defendant was arrested by the police.

2. The defendant challenged his detention on the ground that he was held without probable cause.

3. The answer was filed after the deadline.

4. The complaint was answered with an affirmative defense.

5. Dillon's rule is not recognized by a majority of states.

1. The police arrested the defendant.

2. The defendant challenged his detention on the ground that the police held him without probable cause.

3. The plaintiff filed his answer after the deadline.

4. The defendant raised an affirmative defense to the complaint.

5. A majority of states do not recognize Dillon's Rule.

One last thing: occasionally, passive voice is acceptable. You will notice that we have used passive voice even in this section. Sometimes, passive voice allows you to emphasize a particular idea better. For example, it might be better to say, "The defendant was convicted of robbery," instead of "the court convicted the defendant of robbery," because you may want to focus the reader's attention on the defendant instead of the court. Obviously, there are many other instances where using passive voice is appropriate. However, if you want to produce good legal writing, you should avoid *excessive* use of passive voice.

Precision is Key

Legal writing requires precision. This comes in two key areas of legal writing. First, whenever you describe a rule of law, you should avoid using words that confuse the rule or that create extra elements that are not, in fact, a part of the rule. For example, when the Eighth Amendment forbids "cruel and unusual" punishment, it actually outlaws two things. One term does not subsume the other. The idea is that we presume that all words have a distinct meaning. So some punishments might be cruel, but not unusual, and vice-versa. The Eighth Amendment does not forbid such punishments. It only forbids those punishments that are both cruel *and* unusual. Yet, if, in a rhetorical flourish, you decided to say that the Eighth Amendment forbids punishments that are "cruel, unusual, *and* inhumane," you might cause unnecessary confusion, as you have now added a word for persuasive appeal that a reader could easily mistake as a separate element of the rule.

This is a natural habit. Many legal writers have the temptation to add superfluous words. As the above example demonstrates, by adding superfluous words, you might imply to a reader that the law covers more things than it actually does, or your construction of the legal rule might sound wordy.

As another example, suppose in writing an essay about criminal procedure you said, "A police officer must read a suspect his *Miranda* rights when the suspect is under arrest and in custody." Do you see the problem? The writer may think that he is telling the reader that a person under arrest *is* in custody, but instead, the reader has the impression that the police must *both* have a suspect under arrest *and* in custody to have an obligation to read the suspect his *Miranda* rights. While the two things are arguably different, any distinction is trivial in the context of the rule of law that the writer is trying to propound. So, strike the superfluous words, instead saying, "A police officer must read a suspect his *Miranda* rights when the suspect is in custody." This not only makes the rule of law clearer, but it also makes the sentence shorter. Bar examiners, and lawyers in general, cherish short, concise writing that adequately conveys the legal writer's message.

Avoid Awkward-Sounding Filler Words

For the same reason, you should also avoid using unnecessary, awkward-sounding filler words. For example, writing, "Basically, the law is unconstitutional," is bad style. Just drop the word "basically" altogether—it adds nothing to the sentence. It simply distracts. Here are some more "filler" words and phrases generally to avoid:

- Basically
- Essentially
- In actuality
- In reality
- For all intents and purposes

Also, avoid words that distract from your advocacy in certain contexts. Like "filler" words, these words are a distraction, but in a different way. For instance, when you say words like "clearly" in your advocacy, you suggest to the reader that the contrary view lacks merit. No legal issue would exist if that were the case. So, avoid saying things like, "Clearly, the police had no authority to search the house." Simply remove the word "clearly" and those like it, e.g., "obviously," especially from statements about the core legal issue presented for discussion. If a bar exam question has asked you whether the police had authority to search a house, then the issue is not so clear or obvious.

Use Transitional Words and Phrases

Transitional words and phrases help make sentences cohesive by providing a logical connection. Transition words are easy to identify but are often hard to implement effectively. You should memorize the following transition words and phrases, grouped according to similarity:

- Further, additionally, also, moreover
- Hence, thus, therefore, accordingly, so
- Given that . . . it follows
- Nevertheless, nonetheless, however, in contrast
- Indeed, in fact, of course
- Instead, rather, in contrast

Use these words and phrases to connect sentences together in a thoughtful manner, without using them excessively. Of course, there are always other ways to make sure that sentences logically connect, but these words will help. Further, when you use these words or phrases, make sure to mix them up so your writing does not sound repetitive.

Transitional Words and Phrases Example

> No emergency existed which justified the police officer's warrantless entry of the home. None of the evidence suggests that the violent situation was ongoing; instead, the complaining witness only suggested that her brother struck her once in a fit of rage. Further, the complaining witness never told the police the severity of the situation. Thus, the evidence before the officer failed to demonstrate a *severe, ongoing* emergency justifying a warrantless entry. Therefore, the trial court should suppress the items discovered due to the unlawful entry.

Here is another example. This example demonstrates how to use transitions in explaining the rule statement applicable to the problem presented.

Another Transitional Words and Phrases Example

> If a suspect clearly invokes a right to have counsel present during a custodial interrogation, the police must cease questioning the suspect until counsel is present. Otherwise, the suspect's statements are inadmissible in court. However, the mere mention of an attorney by a suspect does not necessarily invoke the right to have counsel present. The suspect must state his desire to have counsel present so that a reasonable police officer would understand the statement as an actual request to have counsel present. Given this truth, it follows that the suspect's subjective intent is irrelevant.
>
> Here, the suspect may have had the subjective desire to have counsel present, but . . .

Use Ordinals

You can also use ordinals to make your persuasive case in an essay. For example, you might write the following:

Ordinals Example

> The police officer's warrantless entry into the dwelling was unlawful for two reasons. First, none of the evidence suggested that the violent situation was ongoing; instead, the complaining witness only suggested that her brother struck her once in a fit of rage. Second, the complaining witness never told the police the severity of the situation after her brother struck her. Thus, the evidence before the officer failed to demonstrate a severe, ongoing emergency justifying a warrantless entry. Therefore, the trial court should suppress the items discovered due to the unlawful entry.

Ordinals are not for every situation, but on occasion your analysis will simply include a list of successive reasons conducive to the use of ordinals, like the example above.

Dovetailing

As the above examples illustrate, making sure that you have a logical connection and flow between sentences and the ideas that those sentences convey can make all the difference in constructing an excellent essay. This concept is called "dovetailing," and it is a simple yet elusive idea. When sentences dovetail, each successive sentence contains an idea from the last such that the entire essay takes on a more logical, ordered, and persuasive flow. Make sure that your essays contain this key element.

Watch for Split Infinitives

Grammar purists will tell you that split infinitives are grammatically incorrect in all cases. We tend to disagree with that view; in some cases, a split infinitive might sound best.[3] Nevertheless, those cases are rare. Most of the time, you should avoid using them. A split infinitive occurs when you take a verb in the infinitive form and "split" it by adding an adverb in between. For instance, the phrase "to effectively write" is a split infinitive. Instead, you should say, "to write effectively."

Occasionally Use Underlining or Italics for Emphasis

On occasion, you might find that you are emphasizing certain words in your head as you write them down. You can convey that emphasis by underlining the word when handwriting or by *italicizing* the word when typing. This can often be an effective way of communicating your point. Nevertheless, be sure not to use italics too often. When all of the words seem important, *none of them are.*

Use Headings

Headings can be an effective tool for organizing an essay that discusses several different legal issues or different sub-parts of a complex legal issue. For the bar exam, you can easily use headings effectively when a question is divided into several subparts, e.g., parts (a), (b), and (c). In those cases, simply make a heading for each part.

Proofread Repeatedly to Refine Your Writing

Proofread—repeatedly. We cannot emphasize this enough. On test day there will be very little time to proofread and edit your work, but that does not mean you should not do it now. We encourage you to proofread your practice essays at least five times, checking for the things we have

---

[3] For instance, we cannot imagine *Star Trek* without its famous phrase that includes a split infinitive: "To boldly go where no one has gone before."

pointed out in this book and otherwise making your essay a work of art. Eventually, you will begin to notice common mistakes and avoid those mistakes in the future. By doing that, you will not need to proofread your essays *repeatedly* on exam day. You know what they say: practice makes perfect. That is especially true for legal writing, as the difference between good and great writing often shows in the small things.

Final Thoughts

This ends our quick review of some of the more important legal writing issues. In the following chapters, we dive deeper into precisely formulating a full essay. To do that, we will further explore grammar, syntax, and style issues. This is just the beginning of your journey in becoming a better writer and preparing to write homerun essays come exam day.

Should you desire to improve your grammar and style even more, we recommend the following books on legal writing:

- Bryan A. Garner et al., The Redbook: A Manual on Legal Style (2d ed. 2006)
- Bryan A. Garner, Legal Writing in Plain English: A Text with Exercises (2001)
- Bryan A. Garner, The Elements of Legal Style (2d ed. 2002)
- William Strunk, Jr. and E.B. White, The Elements of Style (5th ed. 2008)
- Gregory G. Colomb and Joseph M. Williams, Style: Lessons in Clarity and Grace (10th ed. 2010)

You can also find essay writing tips at http://esqeducation.com.

Chapter Two:
Assessing the Question

Introduction

Your first task in answering any question on the bar exam is to discern what the question is asking. You must assess the correct legal issue the facts describe. To do that, we propose you use something we have dubbed "the linking method." When you use the linking method, you associate key generic facts with specific legal issues and the relevant rule of law. Through lots of practice, you can use this method to quickly identify facts pertinent to the issue that the call of the question is directing you toward.

It is common for bar exam questions to include multiple issues with multiple relevant facts, but for now let us focus on simple questions so that you can acclimate yourself to the linking method.

The Linking Method

To identify the specific legal issue presented in a bar exam question, you must begin by memorizing the relationship between certain facts and the corresponding legal issue. Take the following example:

Criminal Law Fact Pattern

Husband suspects his wife is having an affair with his best friend. Husband begins listening to wife's telephone conversations and overhears her making plans to meet with someone the next evening at a local restaurant. Furious, Husband borrows his neighbor's gun from the neighbor's unlocked garage, with the intention of returning it the next day, and follows his wife to the restaurant. Husband sees his wife having drinks with his best friend and honestly believes his suspicions are true. He pulls out the gun, aims it at his best friend, and pulls the trigger. Unbeknownst to Husband, the neighbor's gun was not loaded. Three men standing near Husband tackle him and hold him until the police arrive.

This question presents several issues and several facts to support each legal issue. If you can memorize key facts that trigger specific legal issues, you will have a significant leg-up on exam day. Here is a chart demonstrating how to link key facts with specific legal issues:

Husband suspects wife of having an affair and follows her with a gun	This fact phrase should trigger the issue of "heat of passion killing" and related *mens rea* issues
Husband borrows neighbor's gun with the intent to return it	This fact phrase should trigger theft crimes, specifically burglary and larceny
Husband aims and shoots a gun at someone	This fact phrase should trigger the issue of attempt and factual impossibility
Three men tackle Husband	This fact phrase should trigger the issue of torts, specifically battery and any defenses such as protection of others
The men hold Husband until the police arrive	This fact phrase should trigger the issue of false imprisonment, although likely inapplicable

This type of relational approach (or "linking method") to bar exam questions will help you identify what the question is *really* asking. It is important not to allow facts that have no relation to the actual legal issue the examiners are testing distract you. For instance, in the above example, the specific questions posed might be as follows:

(a) What is the most severe crime that Husband can be charged with?
(b) Are there any defenses Husband might assert?
(c) Will these defenses succeed?

If presented with these questions, or "calls," you would want to discuss first the crime of attempted murder and list the legal rule for attempted murder. You would then discuss how heat of passion reduces a murder charge to manslaughter and explain whether it is a true defense in this case.

What is the Question Really Asking Me?

You would not want to discuss battery, false imprisonment, burglary, or larceny. Even though there are facts supporting a discussion of these topics, when the call of the question does not address these issues, you should not discuss them. The bar examiners are looking for *specific* answers to the *specific* calls provided to you. Including a discussion of legal issues that they are not asking for, even though you may be correctly stating rules and facts, will not get you credit. After you read the fact pattern, always look at the call of the question and ask, *"What is the question really asking me?"*

Once you get in the habit of associating facts with legal issues, by the time you read the call of the question you will quickly discard the facts and issues that you should not discuss.

Let us try another example with a longer fact pattern:

Civil Procedure/Torts Question

On December 10, 2008, Ted, the owner and operator of a party planning rental business in Little Rock, Arkansas, rented a new fudge fountain to Stan, a wedding planner who was planning an elaborate wedding for his client. Ted also provided the services of his employees to act as servers and to operate the fudge fountain. Ted had purchased the new fountain from Dan, the manufacturer, and had not used it before renting it to Stan.

On March 10, 2008, Gloria, a party planning assistant employed by Stan, was seriously injured while working on site at the wedding venue. The injury occurred when a piece of metal flew off from the fountain and struck her in the eye, causing her to lose her eye. The piece of metal flew off when the pump was turned on by one of Ted's employees.

On April 15, 2011, Gloria commenced an action against Ted in the appropriate trial court to recover damages for her injury. Gloria alleged that a defect in the fountain's pump caused her injury. In the alternative, she alleged that the negligent operation of the machine by Ted's employee caused her injury. Ted's answer consisted of a general denial.

On June 2012, Ted commenced a third-party action against Dan. Ted's third party complaint alleged that the defect in the fountain's pump solely caused Gloria's injury. Therefore, Ted demanded judgment against Dan for the full amount of any judgment that Gloria might recover. Dan's answer consisted of a general denial and that the statute of limitations barred Ted's action.

Gloria's cause of action against Ted and Ted's third party action against Dan were tried together in May 2013 in a jury trial. At trial, Gloria offered proof of her injuries, medical expenses, and lost wages. The only other proof by Gloria was that, while working at the wedding site, a flying piece of metal struck her eye after Ted's employee turned on the fountain pump, causing her injury.

The evidence offered by Ted on his case consisted of uncontroverted proof of Ted's purchase of the new fountain from Dan and the uncontroverted testimony of Ted's employee who was operating the fountain. Ted's employee testified that he was qualified to operate the fudge fountain and that he was operating the fountain in accordance with the manufacturer's operating manual. He further testified that the piece of metal flew off when he turned the pump on. Dan presented no evidence in his defense.

Ted properly moved for judgment dismissing Gloria's complaint on the ground that Gloria had failed to prove a *prima facie* case against Ted. Dan properly moved for judgment dismissing Ted's third party complaint on the grounds that (1) Dan's third party complaint was barred by the statute of limitations and (2) the evidence offered at trial was insufficient to establish a *prima facie* case against Dan. The court denied Ted's motion and denied both branches of Dan's motion.

Before the court submitted the case to the jury, Gloria agreed on the record to settle her case against Ted for $100,000 and Gloria discontinued her action against Dan on the merits. Dan then moved for judgment dismissing Ted's third party complaint against Dan on the ground that the settlement terminated all of Ted's rights against Dan. The court granted Dan's motion.

Were the rulings of the court correct?

Before you get overwhelmed, remember, at this point we are only asking you to identify the appropriate facts, or "fact phrases," and link those fact phrases with the correct legal issues. In this fact pattern, you should identify four issues.

In the space provided, identify the fact phrases and their corresponding issues. Once you are done, compare your answers to our model answers that follow.

First Fact phrase: "Ted duly moved for judgment dismissing Gloria's complaint on the ground that Gloria had failed to prove a *prima facie* case."

Corresponding Issue: Whether the elements for proving a *prima facie* case for negligence and vicarious liability exist.

Second Fact Phrase: "Ted's third party action was barred by the statute of limitations."

Corresponding Issue: Whether the statute of limitations for products liability or manufacturer's defect bars the action in this case.

Third Fact Phrase: "Ted's evidence offered at trial was insufficient to prove a *prima facie* case against Dan."

Corresponding Issue: Whether the trial evidence supports a *prima facie* case.

Fourth Fact Phrase: "[T]he settlement terminated all of Ted's rights against Dan."

Corresponding Issue: Whether the settlement had terminated Ted's rights against Dan.

If you did not get all of the correct fact phrases or the correct issues, do not panic. Many times a long fact pattern will present multiple issues and many facts jumbled together. It is easy to get confused and focus on the incorrect issue. With practice, you will improve. If you failed to get the correct issues, go back through the fact pattern and memorize the fact phrases that trigger the issues discussed, so the next time you see similar language in a fact pattern you will know exactly what issues the examiners are testing.

Let us try one more example:

Uniform Commercial Code (UCC) Question

> Angus told Joe that he had a large gravel yard, much of which was loose rock and clay. Angus was looking for a Caterpillar gravel compactor to make his gravel yard solid enough to use as a parking lot. Joe showed Angus a dirt compactor and said, "This dirt compactor is stronger than the bobcat gravel compactor and will compact anything you roll it over." Angus did a cursory inspection of the dirt compactor and based on Joe's assurances, Angus purchased the dirt compactor. Angus saw the sales tag on the dirt compactor as he was paying for it. The tag stated prominently, "No express warranties; No implied warranty of merchantability." Angus then tried to use the dirt compactor on his gravel yard, and the dirt compactor was unable to compact the loose gravel. Angus was unable to use the gravel yard as a parking lot.
>
> Can Angus bring a breach of warranty claim against Joe under the UCC?

In the space provided, generate fact phrases and link them to the legal issues in this question. **HINT:** even though there is one call in this question and the fact pattern is shorter, there is more than one legal issue to identify. The answers follow below.

How many issues did you identify? If you identified the UCC warranties then you are on the right track. This question asks generally if Angus can assert a claim for breach of warranty. The examiners are testing whether you understand that there are several different warranties under the UCC and that the warranty of "fitness for a particular purpose" provides the strongest claim.

It is also helpful to link phrases like "inspection" with "disclaimer." Even though the call did not specifically ask if a disclaimer applied, since the question gave facts including an inspection, it is appropriate to discuss the legal significance of that inspection.

Developing Your Own Charts

As an example, we have created two charts for two key study areas. These charts are not comprehensive; you should use this as a guide for further creation of your own charts. They will help you significantly in your essay writing preparation.

Fact Phrase	Legal Issue
Sale conditioned on suitability to build on land or suitability of product to perform and then the condition is not met	Mutual mistake and the remedy when rescission occurs
One party knew of a defect and the other party did not	Unilateral mistake and the remedy for unilateral mistake; contract enforceable by the innocent party
Orders placed by phone or fax and confirmed with another merchant's form which contains conflicting terms	Battle of the forms: what terms of the contract prevail? Conflicting terms that do not materially alter the contract are proposed terms and if those proposed terms are not objected to, they become part of the contract. If the conflicting terms materially alter the contract, they fall away and do not become part of the contract
Phone agreements or any oral agreements	Statute of Frauds
Goods sent that do not conform to the order	Non-conforming goods and the remedy for non-conforming goods

Obviously, you can create a chart like the one above for any number of topics. For instance, here are some fact phrases and corresponding issues for Wills:

Any time there is a list of assets and accounts	probate assets vs. non-probate assets and the differences in distribution of the two
Testator hand wrote or any variation of "in the testator's handwriting"	Holographic will? Valid codicil?
It is my intention to change my will or any variation of future intent to execute a will	Discuss valid will execution and why this future intent to create or alter a will does not meet the legal requirements of a valid will
I, Testator, will give you my farm if you leave your job and care for me until my children are grown—or any variation of a contract to dispose of real property (even an oral contract)	This is a contract for a testamentary disposition of real property. In general, contracts must satisfy the statute of frauds. If it is an oral contract it can still be enforceable if: (1) terms of agreement are certain acts in part performance and were made pursuant to the agreement; (2) agreement has been so far performed so that not enforcing it would be fraud on the plaintiff
Omitted spouse or omitted child	Intestacy laws as well as augmented estate law (extra points if you can also memorize the time in which an omitted spouse may make a claim)

Final Thoughts

Try making your own tables of fact phrases and corresponding legal issues for the important subjects in your state. You can make a table for every topic covered in your bar study program and begin linking and memorizing. This will help you when you practice your essay questions. You will find that the more you practice learning which facts trigger a particular legal issue, the simpler answering the bar exam questions will become. In this way, you can help to ensure high marks on the essay portion of the exam.

Chapter Three:
Stating the Issue and Constructing the Rule of Law

Introduction

Now that you have properly assessed the question, it is time to focus on constructing your essay. You will begin with a good statement of the issue (or a conclusion) and a carefully crafted rule of law. Your task is not merely to recite back some bland statement of law so that the grader can say, "Ah, that student has memorized the law." Memorization is certainly a critical part of your success on the bar exam, but it is not enough. An effective essay must *persuade* the grader of the correctness of your position. As a corollary, then, it must also demonstrate that you know and understand how to write in a persuasive manner and, therefore, that you truly understand how the law applies to a certain set of facts.

Set Up the Analysis

Writing a persuasive essay starts with writing a good issue statement and coupling that with a properly constructed rule statement that "sets up" the overtly persuasive portion of your essay. You will not engage in analysis at this stage, but you will *think* about how exactly to communicate the particular rule that you have memorized and appropriately implement those thoughts on paper. Consider the example below.

Criminal Law Question

Adam and Beth live together as boyfriend and girlfriend in Beth's apartment. Adam is a rabid fan of the Cleveland Browns, a professional football team with a less than stellar track record for winning games. Against the better judgment of many sports handicappers, Adam often places bets with his bookie, Carl, that the Browns will win a particular football game. Accordingly, Adam has amassed a substantial debt with Carl, and Carl has threatened to do bad things to Adam if he does not pay off his debt. One day, Adam comes across a box in Beth's closet containing seemingly valuable jewelry. He pawns the jewelry and receives $150 from the pawn shop. However, the jewelry, if sold on the open market, would sell for at least $300, if not more. Beth discovers what Adam has done, kicks him out of her apartment, and calls the police.

The police arrest Adam for grand larceny, and a local state prosecutor later indicts him for the crime. At a bench trial, Adam does not dispute that the value of the jewels exceeds the threshold amount required to convict him of grand larceny. Rather, he argues that he intended to buy the jewels back as soon as he had sufficient funds to do so, which he believed he would have after winning the bet. Assume that the judge, sitting as fact-finder, believes that Adam intended to buy back the jewelry as soon as he was financially able to.

Should the judge find Adam guilty of grand larceny?

You have already learned how to assess the question, but practice makes perfect. Obviously, the issue stands out like a sore thumb: is the defendant guilty of grand larceny? Ah, but that is not quite right. Instead, perhaps the issue is: should the judge find the defendant guilty of grand larceny? However, that leaves out one important fact: given that the judge accepts Adam's testimony that *he intended to buy the jewelry back and return it to Beth once he could afford to do so*, should the judge find Adam guilty of grand larceny? Incidentally, this problem has at least one red-herring: the value of the jewels stolen. Because we are told that Adam stipulates that the amount is enough to satisfy *grand* larceny, you should not address it, except perhaps to say that it is a non-issue.

Now what? Well, your inclination might be to recite the rule about larceny. That is certainly a good start. Larceny is "the taking and carrying away of the personal property of another with the intent to permanently deprive the owner of the property." If you merely put that down in your essay when you recite the rule, you would be missing a lot that you could otherwise say. You should always ask yourself two important questions.

First, "How can I frame the rule in such a way that I have set the stage for the analysis that follows?" Second, "How can I frame the rule in such a way that I focus the grader on the underlying issue presented by the problem?" Using those questions as a guide, consider what you ought to talk about before reading further.

Have you done that? Good! Hopefully, you realized that the question is really about a portion of larceny—the portion focusing on the *mens rea* required of the perpetrator. He must intend to do something very specific—has Adam done that in this case? So, stating both a conclusion and rule statement, you might construct the first half of your essay as follows:

Criminal Law Question – Issue and Rule Statement

> The judge should find Adam guilty of grand larceny, despite his intent to repurchase the jewels as soon as he has the financial ability to do so. Grand larceny is the taking and carrying away of the personal property of another with the intent to permanently deprive the owner of the property, where the property is valued at over $200.[4] A person has the intent to permanently deprive an owner of his property when the person takes the property with the intent to keep the property as his own. This includes those circumstances where the person takes the property, even though he may intend to return the property should some condition prove to be true at some indefinite point in the future.[5]

---

[4] Here, we use the amount applicable in Virginia. Obviously, this amount may be different in your state.

[5] See, e.g., Marsh v. Commonwealth, 57 Va. App. 645, 651-52, 704 S.E.2d 624, 628 (2011) (while a person is not guilty of larceny if he unconditionally intends to return an item, he is guilty if "'he intends to return the property only if he should receive a reward for its return'" (quoting Carter v. Commonwealth, 280 Va. 100, 107, 694 S.E.2d 590, 593 (2010))).

After this paragraph, you would write your formal analysis, which we discuss in Chapter Four.

Write the Rule to Set Up Your Analysis

As you can see, we have already begun the analysis by strategically constructing our rule. While your first inclination may have been to write down the definition of larceny, the better inclination would be to write down a series of interrelated statements that eloquently *narrow* the rule to the ultimate issue. Since we have done that in the example above, our analysis can now focus precisely on the issue the essay presents us with, rather than just broader ideas that do not get to the heart of the question.

Let us try another example.

A Criminal Procedure Example

You are an attorney for a defendant charged with the first-degree murder of his wife. The defendant admits to intentionally killing his wife, but claims he did it in self-defense. You are doubtful of this defense. Nonetheless, he wishes to proceed with this defense at trial.

After the police arrested your client, they took him to an interrogation room where they questioned him about the murder. The police properly read the defendant his *Miranda* rights, and the defendant effectively waived those rights by signing a standardized form. Thereafter, the police asked the defendant whether his wife had provoked him in some way, and the defendant gave no answer. He then sat silently for thirty minutes and faced similar, repeated questioning that sought an incriminating response. Finally, the defendant said, "I want a lawyer." In response, the police said, "OK...well, it's been a while—would you like to use the bathroom?" The defendant agreed and used the bathroom.

When the suspect returned from the bathroom, he explained that he had changed his mind and was willing to answer the police officers' questions. The police asked whether he was sure, and the suspect said that he was. The suspect made it clear that he wanted to speak to the police and that he was willing to do so without a lawyer. He then made incriminating statements inconsistent with self-defense in response to police questioning.

With these facts in mind, you move the court to suppress the incriminating statements. Describe all possible arguments you might make and the likelihood of success.

Spotting the issues in this case will again greatly help you to construct the appropriate rule. See if you can identify the issues and facts, as you did in the previous chapter. Write your answers in the space below, then check them against the model answers we have provided.

_____

_____

_____

_____

_____

_____

_____

_____

_____

_____

_____

_____

_____

_____

_____

_____

_____

Did you spot the issues? Here are the important issues that you should have noticed:

> **Fact Phrase:** "He then sat *silently* for 30 minutes."
>
> **Corresponding Issue:** The defendant may have invoked his right to remain silent.
>
> **Fact Phrase:** The defendant said, "I want a lawyer."
>
> **Corresponding Issue:** The defendant may have invoked his right to counsel.
>
> **Fact phrase:** After the defendant potentially invoked his right to counsel, the police asked him if he wanted to use the bathroom.
>
> **Corresponding Issue:** Did the police impermissibly continue the interrogation?
>
> **Fact phrase:** The defendant "changed his mind."
>
> **Corresponding issue:** Did the defendant reinitiate the interrogation?

Having identified the fact phrases, try writing your issue and rule statements for this problem in the space provided below. Your issue statement here might be a little different because of the broad nature of the question and the multiple issues that arise in the fact pattern. Although bar exam questions will often have distinct, focused sub-questions, you may nevertheless get a question like this one that is more general. Still, remember your purpose: to alert the grader that you have identified not just superficial issues, but the deeper issues that the question is hinting at. Given the number of issues and the way they are presented, you may have to spend more time and space to appropriately set out the issues. A model answer follows on the next page.

Here, is a model way to begin your essay, addressing the issues involved:

Criminal Procedure Example – Issue and Rule Statement

> As defense counsel, I would argue that the law prohibited the police from interrogating the defendant at certain points during the encounter, which should result in the suppression of the defendant's incriminating statements to police. First, I would argue that the defendant invoked his right to remain silent. Second, I would argue that he later invoked his right to have an attorney present.
>
> However, these arguments would be unlikely to succeed. The defendant did not actually invoke his right to remain silent. Further, although he did effectively invoke his right to have counsel present, the police never engaged in any impermissible questioning. Instead, the defendant appears to have re-initiated the interrogation knowingly and voluntarily, and thus continued police interrogation was permissible. Therefore, it is unlikely that these arguments would result in suppression of the defendant's incriminating statements, as I explain in further detail below.

Now try to formulate a rule statement on your own in the space provided. As we have shown above, it might be easiest to approach your rule statement in a linear fashion that corresponds with the relevant events at each stage of the fact pattern. Try doing that yourself. When you are done, consult the model rule statement that follows.

The Fifth Amendment to the U.S. Constitution provides that the government may not compel a person to incriminate himself. This right against self-incrimination is further protected by a series of U.S. Supreme Court cases, most notably *Miranda v. Arizona*. These cases provide certain "prophylactic" rights designed to protect the core Fifth Amendment right against self-incrimination. Among these prophylactic rights are the right to remain silent and the right to have an attorney present during custodial interrogation by police. Although seemingly counter-intuitive, to invoke the right to remain silent a person must actually say that he wishes to remain silent. Similarly, if the person wants an attorney present during a custodial interrogation, the person must ask for one.

Whether a person has effectively invoked either right is judged based upon the "reasonable police officer" standard. If a reasonable police officer would have understood a statement from the defendant as requesting the protection of either right, then the defendant effectively invoked his right and any statements made in response to police interrogation are inadmissible. This standard is used because the purpose of the prophylactic protections adopted by the Supreme Court is to deter police misconduct. In that vein, case law does not prohibit all police questioning after a suspect invokes his right to remain silent or the right to an attorney. Only those questions designed to illicit an incriminating response are prohibited. Further, police may ask such questions *if* the person in custody knowingly and voluntarily reinitiates the interrogation.

Ok, that was a big one, but it is important for you to have the ability to thoroughly explain the complex rules relevant to a particular problem. Now that you have conquered that, take a little time to review the law, and when you are ready to come back, we will show you how to apply the law to the facts in an effective manner.

Chapter Four: Analysis

Introduction

In the last chapter, you learned how to set up the issue statement properly and to explain the rule fully, narrowing the rule to suit the issue and to hone in on the analysis to follow. In this chapter, you take the next step by learning how to write effective analysis that will impress the bar examiners.

In the analysis, your answer comes alive. It ties everything together. Where a conventional answer might just regurgitate facts, your answer will persuasively tie your rule explanation and the facts together and drive the grader to one compelling answer: your answer.

Note Important Facts

As you first read an essay question, underline important facts that trigger a rule and narrowed explanations of the rule, as we have previously discussed. You will use these facts to construct your analysis.[6]

Once you have underlined which facts are relevant, you can then determine which facts need to be in your analysis. For example, suppose you are given a contract question and the call of the question is: "What claims and defenses may each party assert against the other?" With that call, you should look for facts related to breach, warranty, damages, statute of limitations, non-performance, excuse, and other relevant issues.

---

[6] If you want to try something really advanced, also make note of unimportant facts. Try circling these facts while underlining important facts. If you have the opportunity, you can quickly mention in the analysis why the reader should ignore a particular fact. Be careful with this technique—you should not use it too much. However, appropriately calling out a particularly tricky fact for the trick that it is may really impress your grader.

Suppose there are facts that support a non-contract claim, like trespass. Ignore these facts as it relates to this specific call. It is quite possible, even likely, that you will see facts that have nothing to do with the call or calls you are confronted with. Do not be thrown by multiple issues. Focus on the issue that the call of the question is driving at. The bar examiners will give you hints as to what they want you to discuss. For instance, take the following question.

Contract Question

> Homeowner hired painter to paint a house. The painter fell behind on his painting schedule due to heavy rain. The painter could have hired additional help, but did not because it would be too expensive. The painter did not finish painting the house that Homeowner hired painter to paint.
>
> Does the painter have a legal excuse for his contract breach?

Contract Question Explanation

Go with your gut: this is an impracticability issue. So, talk about the issue of impracticality; do not spend twenty minutes discussing contract formation and breach. The call of the question already assumes these things as true.

Also, recall the lessons we covered in the last chapter. As you memorize rules, you should have a good idea how you will generally write those rules down, at least in their general form. These "starter sentences" will set you up for success on test day. For example, given a contract question where the issue is impracticability, as here, a good starter sentence might be, "A party may be excused if his performance becomes impracticable due to unforeseen difficulties." As discussed earlier, you may need to further narrow and explain the rule. In some cases, your rule statement will be short, and in other cases, it may not. Always remember to use your best judgment.

What do you do with the facts next? *Do not just list them in your essay.* For example, do not write, "Here, the painter could not finish the job because there was heavy rain and hiring more employees would be too expensive." This does not show the examiners that you fully understand the relationship between the law and the facts. Instead, use the techniques we have already reflected on to apply those facts effectively to your rule that you stated in your starter sentence. For example, write the following *complete* model answer.

Contract Question – Complete Model Answer

> The painter has no legal excuse for his breach. The law will excuse a contract party from his performance if his performance becomes impracticable due to unforeseen difficulties. An obligation becomes impracticable only in extreme cases. In this case, the rain was an unforeseen difficulty that delayed the painter. However, the painter could have hired additional employees—even if the cost was high—and completed the painting job. The performance of a contract obligation is not impracticable simply because performing that obligation would create a loss. The law does not recognize such a state of affairs as an extreme condition excusing contract performance. Therefore, the painter is not excused due to impracticability, and thus he has no defense to his breach.

Note how the model answer uses the facts to highlight the rule. It demonstrates to the grader that you really know how that rule applies, not just that you have a rule memorized.

Let us continue with a full contract question. Use the sample paragraph above to shape your answer. Remember to underline key facts, link the fact to the rule, properly state the rule, and then use a starter sentence.

Second Contract Question

On July 1, 2006, Owner signed a contract with Perfect Painter to paint the exterior of Owner's house by September 1, 2006, for a contract price of $5,000. On August 1, Owner called Perfect by telephone and told him that it was very important that he paint the house by September 1, 2006 because he was moving and needed to sell his house in September.

The weather was extremely rainy and Perfect fell behind on all of his painting jobs. Perfect could have hired more employees to help catch him up on his painting jobs. Had he done this, Perfect would have lost money, so he did not hire additional help. Perfect only painted half of Owner's house by September 15, 2006 and did not complete the job until September 30, 2006. Owner could not sell his house in September.

Owner decided to move anyway, and left his house vacant for three months until he finally put it on the market and sold it March 1, 2007. Realtor told Owner that the selling season runs from February through April. This is well-known in the real estate industry.

Owner has refused to pay Perfect for the work he did because he did not perform the work on time. Perfect has sued Owner for $5,000. Owner denies liability and counter claims against Perfect for the interest Owner had to pay on his mortgage because he could not sell his house until March 1, 2007.

What claims and defenses may Owner and Perfect reasonably assert against each other, and what is the likelihood of success on each?

Write your answer on a separate sheet of paper. When you are done, you will find model analysis paragraphs below. (**Hint:** Use headings as outlined in Chapter 1. Organize by party opponents first, e.g., Owner v. Perfect. Under each of these headings, explain the claims and defenses each can bring.)

How did you do? Compare your answers to the model analysis paragraphs that follow. We have also included relevant rules.

Second Contract Question - Model Analysis

Owner v. Perfect

Breach of contract: A written contract for services to be performed by a specific date is breached if those services are not completely performed by the written and agreed upon date.

Analysis:

Here, the contract stated that Perfect had to paint Owner's house by September 1, 2006. Perfect failed to paint Owner's house by the specified date. Therefore, Owner can assert a claim for breach of contract against Perfect.

Defense

Time is of the essence: The contract should generally contain language stating that time is of the essence for contracts for performance of services. If no such language is stated in the contract, then a reasonable time is permitted.

Analysis:

In this case, time was not made of the essence in the written contract. Perfect completed the work on September 30 instead of

September 1. 29 days is a reasonable time to perform painting services. Thus, Perfect did not materially breach the contract.

Impracticability: A party may be excused if his performance becomes impracticable due to unforeseen circumstances. Unforeseen circumstances are unforeseen difficulties whose risk either party could not have or did not assume. Mere economic loss does not create an impracticable circumstance.

Analysis:

Here, Perfect will argue that it was impracticable for him to complete the painting job by August 1. He will claim that the heavy rain delayed his ability to complete the painting. This defense will not be successful because Perfect could have hired additional help in order to complete the painting job and economic loss does not create impracticability. Thus, Perfect will be unsuccessful with this defense.

Always remember that when you have a contract question, there will be some measure of damages. Your answer should make sure to address what damages each party is likely to recover.

In general, the amount a party can recover is the amount that will put the non-breaching party in the same position he would have been in if the breach had not occurred. Further, the non-breaching party has a duty to mitigate if possible.

In this case, Perfect delayed finishing the job by 29 days. It was unforeseeable that this delay would cause the Owner's house not to sell. Therefore, Perfect will be liable for breach of contract if the court finds that he materially breached the painting contract, but he will not be liable for any damages resulting from Owner not selling his house at the time he expected.

Perfect v. Owner

Substantial performance: When a party substantially performs his portion of the contract, he is entitled to recover for that substantial performance.

Analysis:

Here, Perfect will likely recover the contract price for painting the house since he completed painting the house. Further, he will assert that no "time is of the essence" language appeared in the contract. Thus, the fact that his performance was late is not substantial and he is entitled to recover the contract price for the painting of the house.

Unjust enrichment: A party may recover for unjust enrichment when he confers a benefit on another and where such benefit should be reasonably compensated, but the benefiting party fails to pay compensation.

Analysis:

Here, Perfect conferred a benefit of a newly painted house on Owner. This is a benefit that Perfect reasonably expected to be compensated for. Thus, Owner, by not paying Perfect, is unjustly enriched. Accordingly, Perfect is entitled to recover damages equal to the benefit conferred, which in this case would be the contract price.

That was a big question, but you should be prepared for such questions. Let us walk through another question.

Federal Jurisdiction Question

Allison sues Ben in federal court for an injury that Allison sustained from an accident that Allison alleges Ben negligently caused. Allison further reasonably and specifically alleges that she sustained medical bills of $50,000, property damage of $3,000, and pain and suffering valued at $20,000 resulting directly from the accident. Allison also alleges that months after the accident, Ben intentionally punched her during settlement negotiations because he was upset with the situation. The punch displaced Allison's jaw, which a doctor had to re-set. Allison has therefore also included a separate claim for damages extending from this incident in the amount of $2,000 for medical bills and $1,000 for pain and suffering.

The initial accident occurred in New York, while the incident during settlement discussions occurred in Pennsylvania, approximately halfway between New York and Maryland. Allison is a citizen of New York, while Ben was merely visiting New York at the time of the accident. Ben is a citizen of Maryland. At the time Allison filed suit, Allison was living at her home in New York, while Ben was in New York on business at that time.

Ben moves to dismiss the federal suit for lack of subject matter jurisdiction. Will Ben prevail on the motion? Assume that all the states in question recognize the claims and damages asserted in the suit, and that nothing beyond the pleadings are before the court.

This question presents us with a perfect opportunity to tie together all of the concepts we have reviewed thus far. Try writing a *complete* answer to this question on a separate sheet of paper. You will find a discussion of the problem and a model answer below.

Hopefully, you did *not* write something like the following:

> Allison lives in New York and Ben lives in Maryland. Both parties are domiciled in different states. Because both parties are domiciled in different states, they are diverse parties and so diversity jurisdiction is proper.

This approach will not get you the points that you need. In the above example, there is no rule statement. There is no clear demonstration that you understand what diversity jurisdiction or subject matter jurisdiction means. In fact, this answer barely scratches the surface on the more specific issues raised by this question. Although the conclusion is ultimately correct, this approach is unlikely to gain you many points.

Instead, remember to start by identifying the issue and constructing a rule statement and explanation that sets up your analysis. The analysis section of your essay is the only place the facts in the essay should appear. However, remember that you should not just put down some bland listing of facts. Tie your rule in with the facts so that your essay compels the grader to agree with your conclusion and convinces him that you fully understand the legal concepts at play. This mindset will ensure maximum points on the exam.

A complete answer to this question should look something like this. You can generally use paragraphs as we have—to divide the distinct statements and explanations—although you should ultimately use your best judgment on when to start a new paragraph for any given answer.

Federal Jurisdiction – Complete Answer

Ben will not prevail on the motion.

Federal courts have subject matter jurisdiction over all civil actions where the amount in controversy exceeds $75,000 and is between citizens of different states. The location of the parties at any particular time is irrelevant for determining diversity of citizenship—only the parties' citizenship *at the time plaintiff files suit* matters. Moreover, the amount in controversy need not come from a single claim. The law permits a single plaintiff to aggregate claims arising under its diversity jurisdiction in order to reach the amount in controversy required.

Here, Allison was a citizen of New York and Ben was a citizen of Maryland at the time Allison filed suit. It is of no consequence where Allison and Ben were physically located at any particular time before, during, or after the filing of the lawsuit. Only their citizenship at the time Allison filed suit controls. Thus, since Ben and Allison are from different states, they have diverse citizenship.

The question remains whether the amount in controversy satisfies the requirements of the law. In this case, Allison's claims for negligence and battery both rely upon diversity jurisdiction for relief in federal court, and thus she may aggregate her claims. When added together, her claims amount to $76,000, satisfying the requirement that they exceed $75,000. Accordingly, her suit also satisfies the amount in controversy requirement.

Because Ben and Allison have diverse citizenship and Allison's suit exceeds the amount in controversy requirement, federal diversity jurisdiction exists. Therefore, Ben's motion will fail.

Now that you have tried a relatively simple question, try your hand at a more involved question. Write your answer to the question on a separate sheet of paper. A complete answer follows the question.

Wills Question

John Smith ("husband") provides the following in a validly executed will:

"I, John Smith, leave my entire estate to my wife, or if she should die before me, I leave my entire estate to my son and my daughter to share equally."

John Smith's wife, Jane Smith, provides the following in a validly executed will:

"I, Jane Smith, leave my entire estate to my husband."

John and Jane Smith are both killed in a car accident. The car accident was caused when son tampered with the brakes of his father's car such that they would not work when his father was driving. When the police arrived on the scene, Jane was in the passenger side with her seatbelt still fastened. John was outside the car a few feet from the car and it appeared he had opened the driver's door and was attempting to crawl to the side to help his wife.

The son claims he was trying to fix his father's brakes and did not intentionally sever the brake line. The police investigated but found no concrete evidence to prosecute the son for a criminal act.

This jurisdiction has adopted the Uniform Simultaneous Death Act. Both wills have been submitted to a probate court having proper jurisdiction.

(a) How should the probate court distribute husband's estate?
(b) How should the probate court distribute wife's estate?

Remember, when beginning an essay question, think of the general rule the examiners are testing and begin with that.

Wills Example – Complete Answer

Husband's Estate:

Son and daughter will inherit husband's estate equally.

<u>Simultaneous Death Act</u>

The simultaneous death act requires the beneficiary of a will to survive a testator by 120 hours. Otherwise, the law considers the beneficiary to have pre-deceased the testator. In this case, the husband appears to have died after the wife, since the police found him outside the vehicle and the police found the wife still fastened inside the vehicle. The Act requires a beneficiary to survive a testator by 120 hours, yet the police found both husband and wife dead at the scene when they arrived. Thus, the state of the scene of the accident suggests that the wife did not survive husband by 120 hours. Accordingly, wife pre-deceased husband, and therefore the husband's estate passes equally to his son and daughter as stipulated in the husband's will.

<u>Slayer Statute</u>

A beneficiary cannot take from a will if a preponderance of the evidence establishes that the beneficiary intentionally killed the testator. In contrast, a criminal charge of homicide requires proof beyond a reasonable doubt to convict. Thus, the proof required to invoke the slayer statute is significantly less than the proof required to convict a person of the underlying crime of homicide.

In this case, it is true that the son has not been charged with homicide. There is evidence to support an innocent reason as well as a malicious reason for the damage to the car's brakes. At best, then, the evidence is in equipoise. Yet, to meet the preponderance of the evidence, it must be more likely than not that the son intentionally damaged the brakes. Thus, the facts do not support the evidentiary standard required. Therefore, the Slayer Statute does not bar the son from collecting his share of the inheritance. Additional evidence is required to tip the scales in favor of barring the son under the statute.

Wife's Estate:

Son and daughter will also inherit the wife's estate equally.

Just as the wife did not survive the husband by 120 hours, so too husband did not survive wife by 120 hours. For the same reason as before, the husband will not be treated as having survived the wife. Therefore, the wife's estate will pass directly to the son and daughter equally.

As you can see, this question asked you to identify two main issues: the Simultaneous Death Act and the Slayer Statute. It may seem obvious, but if the examiners give you an act or statute that you are to apply, *they are most likely testing you on that statute or act.* Do not be fooled into thinking it is a trick question!

Let us try another example.

Business Law Question

Owen, the owner of a funeral home, wanted to purchase 100 caskets from Corey Coffin, a distributor of funeral caskets. Owen's funeral home was a family business, so his 17-year-old son Art would often work with him to learn the trade. Owen decided to give Art more responsibility and asked him to place the casket order with Corey, but only with Corey since Owen had purchased from him in the past. Art was excited about the opportunity and on March 1, 2010, Art entered into a signed written contract with Corey for the purchase of 100 caskets at $1,000 for a total contract price of $100,000.

Art wanted to impress his father, so Art, without his father's approval, decided to look for better prices on caskets and found Darren Dealer who would sell him 100 caskets for 50,000. Not wanting to miss this great deal, Art immediately entered into another signed contract with Darren for 100 caskets at $500 each for a total contract price of $50,000. Art put in the contract that his father gave him full permission to enter into any purchase agreement.

On March 15, 2010, Art sent his father, Owen, the contracts he entered into with Corey and Darren. On March 20, 2010, Art received a letter from Owen that he accepted both contracts.

On April 1, 2010, Corey notified Owen that he would not deliver the caskets because he had found out that Art was a minor and he did not do business with children. The next day, Darren advised Owen that he would not fulfill his contract because he learned that Art had no authority to act on his own in signing the contract.

What can Owen do, if anything, to enforce the contracts against Corey and Darren?

Write your answer on a separate sheet of paper. Remember to use headings to assess the rights and remedies against each individual. A model answer follows, along with an explanation.

Business Law Question – Complete Answer

Owen v. Corey

Owen can enforce the contract even though Art, a minor, entered into the contract as Owen's agent.

A minor can act as an agent of a principal and as such has the same authority and capacity as the principal. To act as an agent of the principal, the agent must act within the scope of authority granted to him by the principal. A contract entered into by a minor is voidable by the minor and not by the other contracting party.

In this case, Owen, as principal, gave Art the authority to act as his agent by expressly stating Art has the authority and responsibility to place the order for caskets with Corey. Thus, Art was acting as an agent of Owen within the scope of authority expressed by the principal. Corey may not raise the defense of Art's minority, since only Art may raise this defense. Therefore, Owen can enforce the contract with Corey.

Owen v. Darren

Owen cannot enforce the contract because Art made a fraudulent misrepresentation of a material fact to Darren.

A fraudulent misrepresentation of a material fact voids a contract. In general, if a party makes a knowingly false representation of a material fact with the intent to induce another party to enter into a contract, the contract is void.

Darren will argue the contract should not be enforced because Art represented that he had the full permission of his father, Owen, to enter into any purchase agreement and that his statement was fraudulent. In this case, Art did make a fraudulent statement and he made the statement with the intent to induce Darren to enter into a contract and the authority to enter into a contract is a material fact, thus it is possible to show real fraud and therefore the contract is void.

Business Law Question – Explanation

This question is really testing agency and minor capacity as well as fraudulent misrepresentation. If you concluded that no real fraud could be shown because you thought Art may have believed he had the authority to enter into purchase agreements, or that Art did not make the statement to induce Darren to enter into the contract, you would likely still get full credit.

The key is to state the rule completely and use the facts to support your conclusion. If you have the essential elements in your answer and you write your answer well, you should get significant credit regardless of your conclusion.

Final Thoughts

You began your journey with some basics and have now concluded with well-written, complete answers. You should be very proud of your progress thus far. You should continue practicing the concepts you have learned in these preceding chapters as you prepare to tackle the wealth of material provided by your comprehensive study course. Chapter 5 provides you with more practice questions. Before we move on to that chapter, let us review what we have learned so far.

Identify the issue by identifying important facts and matching those with memorized rule statements. State the issue in a meaningful way; do not regurgitate the question. Sometimes, you should write a definitive conclusion; other times, you may wish to state the issue without concluding things up front.

When you write the rule, you must put the rule in context for the grader. Start with a good general rule to start on the right foot. Then, further explain the rule by narrowing it to the particular facts and issues presented. By doing this, you set the stage for your analysis that will follow.

When you write your analysis, remember to place your facts in context. Juxtapose the facts to the law and discuss the interplay between the two to drive to the conclusion. If you merely string a list of facts together and then make a conclusion, you have not properly used each fact to explain how the law applies and how you have arrived at your conclusion. Avoid that kind of cursory analysis and drive your point home. Otherwise, you will lose crucial points on test day.

In the next chapter, we provide you with several additional examples with which to practice this method.

Chapter Five:
Practice Makes Perfect

Introduction

This chapter is designed to give you additional practice writing bar exam essays. We have based the questions in this chapter from issues tested on the Virginia bar exam over the past ten years. We have included model answers as a point of comparison. The model answers are certainly not the only good answers to the questions presented in this Chapter. Nevertheless, through practice, you should try to conform your writing style to the style found in the model answers.

Directions

You can do the first two or three essays untimed, if you so choose. Try not to consult any outside materials, unless you have difficulty recalling the law. If you do, set the problem aside, review the law, then return to the problem; do not use outside materials while writing the problem. We would like you to get accustomed to constructing your rules independently. Once you have done two or three problems untimed, try timing yourself. Each question indicates the time you should take. If you cannot write the essay in the time provided, try writing it in no more than thirty-five minutes.

Question 1: Federal Procedure

An employee of a medium-sized industrial business in Midlothian, Virginia has sued the business in federal district court, claiming that the business discriminated against him in employment decisions based on his race. You are the business' attorney. The business has not previously confronted allegations of racial discrimination. In fact, it has no policy in place regarding what to do if such allegations arise. You have decided to investigate the matter by employing an outside consultant. The consultant interviews the employee's direct supervisor, and makes a written transcript of the conversation. Meanwhile, the employee's counsel finds out about this interview and wishes to obtain the transcript produced by the consultant in discovery. The supervisor remains available for further inquiries from either party. In the face of an appropriate discovery request, must you turn over the transcript to the employee or his counsel?

Write your answer on a separate sheet of paper. If you are timing yourself, take no more than *twenty minutes* to answer this question.

Question 1 Answer

The attorney does not need to turn over the transcript to the employee or his counsel.

Generally, an attorney's work product is not subject to discovery, nor is the work product of his agents. However, for this rule to adhere, the attorney or his agent must have prepared the document in anticipation of litigation. A document prepared in the normal course of business is subject to discovery. Moreover, a party may obtain discovery of any document prepared in anticipation of litigation if the party seeking discovery can show that the document is otherwise discoverable and that he is unable to obtain the document or its substantial equivalent without undue hardship.[7]

Here, the consultant, as my agent, has interviewed the employee's supervisor and has prepared a transcript of the interview *in anticipation of litigation*. I did not direct him to interview the supervisor as part of a regular business practice; in fact, *no policy exists* on the matter. Moreover, without something more, opposing counsel cannot show undue hardship, as he can simply interview the supervisor himself. Accordingly, the transcript is not discoverable.

---

[7] Federal Rule of Civil Procedure 26(b)(3) provides further details.

Question 2: Choice of Law

A car accident occurs in New York. Michael, a New York resident, was the driver of the first car. Boz, the driver of the second car, is a Virginia resident. Boz and Michael both negligently failed to stop at a stop sign. The accident occurred exactly two years ago. New York has a one-year statute of limitations on personal injury cases. Michael files a personal injury claim in Virginia, claiming that Boz negligently caused the accident and Michael's resulting injuries. Boz raises the statute of limitations as a defense, claiming that New York law applies and that its statute of limitations bars the action. He also raises Michael's negligence as a defense. Boz does not object to jurisdiction or venue.

(a) Will Boz prevail in his defense based on the statute of limitations?
(b) If Boz is right that Michael was negligent, what effect will that have on Michael's action?

Write your answer on a separate sheet of paper. If you are timing yourself, take no more than *thirty-five minutes* to answer this question.

Question 2 Answer

Call A

Boz will not prevail in his statute of limitations defense. Virginia applies a traditional approach to choice of law issues. Accordingly, Virginia will apply its own procedural rules to the case, and the substantive law of the state where the cause of action arose. Generally, the statute of limitations is a procedural rule, with certain narrow exceptions inapplicable here. Thus, Virginia will apply its own statute of limitations to this case, which is two years for personal injury claims. Here, Michael filed his claim within the two years required of the statute of limitations. Therefore, Boz will not prevail in his statute of limitations defense.

Call B

If Boz is right that Michael was negligent, this will bar his claim because Virginia is a contributory negligence state. As stated above, the *substantive* law of Virginia controls an action brought in a Virginia court. In Virginia, a person cannot recover in a negligence action if the person was negligent to *any* degree. Thus, if Boz is right about Michael's negligence, that negligence bars his action.

Question 3: Wills

An elderly woman asks a friend to take care of her until she passes. She promises to leave him the house if he will quit his job and care for her. The friend quits his job and cares for the woman for the next four years. The woman then meets a man she wishes to marry. She signs a document purporting to be her will, leaving everything—including the house—to the new man upon her death. The document is entirely in her handwriting. No one witnesses her sign this document. The elderly woman dies the next day.

(a) Is the document a valid will?

(b) Assuming the woman made a valid will, can the friend enforce the promise and receive the house? Assume the friend can sufficiently prove the existence of the agreement and his performance in compliance with the agreement to the satisfaction of a court. Fully explain your answer.

Write your answer on a separate sheet of paper. If you are timing yourself, take no more than *forty minutes* to answer this question.

Question 3 Answer

<u>Call A</u>

The document is a valid will.

Ordinarily, for a document to be a valid will, the document must be (1) a testamentary disposition, (2) in writing, (3) signed by the testator, and (4) signed by two witnesses in the presence of the testator. By their signatures, the witnesses are acknowledging either that they witnessed the testator sign the document or that the testator acknowledged to them that the signature on the document was his. However, a testator may circumvent some of these requirements by the creation of a holographic will. A holographic will is a testamentary document wholly in the handwriting of the testator and signed by him. Two disinterested witnesses must later testify at probate that the document is wholly in the handwriting of the testator.

Here, the document is testamentary—i.e., it directs the disposition of her belongings upon her death. Further, it is wholly in the woman's handwriting and signed by her. Therefore, the document is a valid will.

<u>Call B</u>

Yes, the friend can enforce the promise and receive the house, despite the fact that the promise was not made in writing and despite the fact that the woman bequeathed the house to the man in her will.

In general, contracts for the disposition of real estate must satisfy the statute of frauds. However, an oral agreement to devise real estate is specifically enforceable in equity if:

(1)   the terms of the agreement are certain and definite, based on valuable consideration,

(2)   an act in partial performance refers to or was made pursuant to the agreement, and

(3)   the agreement has been so far performed that refusal of execution of the agreement would operate as a fraud on the plaintiff.

Nonetheless, a court sitting in probate over a valid will in conflict with an outside, enforceable agreement will still execute the terms of the will. Thus, it is incumbent upon the party to the agreement to enforce the agreement in a separate court action. In the case of an agreement to convey real estate, a court sitting will generally require specific performance, because a legal remedy, i.e., monetary damages, is insufficient to make an aggrieved party whole. Thus, to achieve this remedy, the court in the separate action will construe the devisee of the real estate as directed by the will as holding the real estate in a constructive trust for the benefit of the party seeking enforcement of the agreement.

Here, the friend should be able to overcome the statute of frauds and enforce the oral agreement, assuming that he can sufficiently prove the existence of the agreement between him and the woman and his fulfillment of the terms of the agreement. The agreement has certain and definite terms—a promise by the woman to give the friend the house in exchange for a promise by the man to quit his job and take care of her until she dies. As with any contract, "to take care of" someone is a sufficiently definite term because it presumes an objectively reasonable interpretation, even though on its face it may seem in some ways indefinite. Moreover, the friend has performed his part of the agreement, and he would have a fraud acted against him otherwise, as he quit his job and presumably suffered considerable hardship to take care of the woman, only to have the woman hand the property over to another person. As explained above, the friend should have recourse in equity under these circumstances, and thus he should be able to obtain the house.

Question 4: Virginia Civil Procedure & Torts

A man and his friend attended a baseball game one night in Norfolk, Virginia. The game was exciting and the fans were expecting a particular player to hit a home run. The player stepped up to bat and hit a ball down the third base line, over the wall and into the stands where the man and friend were seated. The friend jumped up and raised his hands in an attempt to catch the home run ball. As he jumped, his elbow accidentally struck the man in the eye, causing a black eye. The man sues the friend for battery in general district court in Norfolk.

(a) During discovery, the man serves 35 interrogatories on the friend. He fails to get leave of court. May the man do this?

(b) After discovery, the friend files a motion for summary judgment. The pleadings dispute whether the friend intended to strike the man. In the depositions of the man and the friend, both testified that the friend did not intentionally strike the man. However, no written admissions on this fact are before the court. Is the friend entitled to summary judgment?

Write your answer on a separate sheet of paper. If you are timing yourself, take no more than *twenty-five minutes* to answer this question.

Question 4 Answer

<u>Call A</u>

The man may not serve 35 interrogatories without leave of court. A party may serve up to thirty interrogatories on an opposing party, without leave of court, in Virginia. However, leave of court is required to serve beyond this amount. Thus, to serve 35 interrogatories, the man must get leave of court.

<u>Call B</u>

The friend is not entitled to summary judgment. At any time after the parties have filed all pleadings, any party may move for summary judgment. In Virginia, a movant is entitled to summary judgment on a cause of action if there are no questions of material fact genuinely in dispute and the movant is entitled to judgment as a matter of law on the action. To determine whether a party is entitled to summary judgment, a court may look to the pleadings, admissions, and any orders made pursuant to the pre-trial conference. Here, the pleadings dispute whether the friend intentionally struck the man. Although the depositions show no dispute exists, the trial court may not consider depositions to resolve a motion for summary judgment. The court may rely only on the pleadings here, and those pleadings demonstrate a dispute of material fact. Therefore, the friend is not entitled to summary judgment.

Question 5: Professional Responsibility

Dan negligently strikes Cindy with his car as Cindy is crossing the street. Cindy hires an attorney. The attorney knows that Dan carries significant liability insurance that would pay for Cindy's damages. The attorney calls Dan and says, "I know you had drugs in your pocket when you struck Cindy. I could turn you in to the police for drug possession, but I won't do that if you agree to settle." Dan refuses to settle. The attorney investigates the matter further and discovers video tape surveillance that shows Dan was talking on his cell phone when he struck Cindy in a clearly marked crosswalk. The attorney has filed the suit to gain a judgment for his client or to force a settlement.

   (a) Has the attorney violated any professional rules of conduct?
   (b) Dan hires his best friend, whom Dan has known all his life, to defend the suit. The friend is a licensed Virginia attorney. Dan tells his friend about the threat of criminal prosecution made by Cindy's attorney. The friend has never known Dan to lie, and he believes Dan. What ethical obligation, if any, does the friend have regarding the threat?

Write your answer on a separate sheet of paper. If you are timing yourself, take no more than *thirty minutes* to answer this question.

Question 5 Answer

Call A

Two rules are conceivably applicable to the attorneys' conduct, and the attorney has violated one of the rules. A lawyer may not present or threaten to present criminal charges solely to obtain an advantage in a civil matter. Moreover, an attorney may not file a frivolous action. An action is frivolous, even though there is good-faith belief that it will be successful, if it is brought based on an improper motive, i.e., it is used to harass, delay, or embarrass. Here, the attorney has violated the rules by threatening criminal action to gain advantage in a civil matter, and thus he has violated the rules. However, the action itself is not frivolous. The filing of the suit is not intended to harass, delay, or embarrass, but instead to gain money the client is legitimately owed, since the evidence establishes a good-faith claim for money damages based on negligence. Therefore, the attorney has violated one of two conceivably applicable rules.

Call B

Dan's friend has an ethical obligation to report Cindy's attorney to the Virginia State Bar. The Rules of Professional Conduct require a lawyer having reliable information that another lawyer has committed a violation of the Rules or that raises a substantial question as to that lawyer's honesty to inform the appropriate authority. Here, the friend has reliable information of a violation of the rules by another attorney. The friend has known Dan all his life and knows Dan to be trustworthy. Further, he believes Dan's account of the threat made by Cindy's attorney. This qualifies as reliable information—the friend need not have first-hand knowledge of the violation, but merely reliable information. Therefore, the friend has a duty to report the threat made by Cindy's attorney to the Virginia State Bar.

Question 6: Criminal Law and Procedure

John is a low-level member of a criminal street gang. He and another member of the gang, Steve, decide to rob a convenience store together. They both "scope out" the store and jointly determine the best time to rob it. They also decide to both wear ski masks and gloves, and to arm themselves with guns for use during the robbery. They plan to go into the store together. Because Steve is a convicted felon, John buys him a gun from a gun shop and gives the gun to Steve. John also buys two ski masks and two pairs of gloves and gives one of each to Steve. John and Steve then drive over to the convenience store together. Steve gets out of the car and approaches the store. John has a change of heart and refuses to go inside the store. Nonetheless, Steve enters the store and threatens the clerk with the gun John gave him. Because of this threat, the clerk gives Steve $200 from the store's cash register. Steve then jumps in the car and John drives off. Days later, police arrest Steve based on information from the clerk. By interrogating Steve, they find out about John's involvement, and arrest him too.

The local prosecuting attorney, or Commonwealth's attorney, indicts John for robbery. During his case-in-chief, the prosecutor introduces indisputable evidence of all of John's actions related to the robbery of the convenience store. John moves to strike the indictment, arguing that he did not actually rob the clerk.

(a) Will John prevail in his motion to strike?

(b) Suppose John is acquitted of the robbery charge, which prompts the prosecutor to bring new charges of conspiracy to commit robbery. John motions the court to dismiss the charge based on the double jeopardy clause of the Fifth Amendment to the U.S. Constitution. Will John prevail in the motion?

(c) Suppose John loses the motion to dismiss the charge based on double jeopardy and is convicted in circuit court of conspiracy to commit robbery. The court sentences him and enters a final order. He wishes to appeal this order. To what court should John appeal?

Write your answer on a separate sheet of paper. If you are timing yourself, take no more than *thirty-five minutes* to answer this question.

Question 6 Answer

<u>Call A</u>

    John will not prevail in his motion to strike because he is a principal in the second degree to the robbery. In Virginia, all indictments for a crime include an indictment for the commission of the crime as a principal in the second degree. A person is guilty of robbery as a principal in the first degree if he takes the property of another by force, threat of force, or intimidation. A person is guilty of a crime as a principal in the second degree if he aids, abets, counsels, or commands the commission of a crime by another. Although John is not a principal in the first degree to the robbery, he is a principal in the second degree. He aided and abetted the robbery ultimately committed by Steve by acquiring a gun, ski mask, and gloves for Steve, and by serving as the getaway driver. John knew the illegal purpose for which Steve would use these items and that he was helping John flee the scene. Thus, even though John ultimately decided not to directly participate in the crime by entering the store, his aid of Steve was sufficient to make him a principal in the second degree to the robbery. Thus, his motion to strike will fail.

<u>Call B</u>

    John will not prevail on the motion because the crimes of robbery and conspiracy to commit robbery are distinct crimes that do not conflict with the double-jeopardy clause. The double jeopardy clause generally precludes the conduct of two trials for the same offense. Thus, as set out by the U.S. Supreme Court in its *Blockburger* test, double jeopardy does not apply where each offense has an element that the other does not. This test is satisfied in this case. To convict a person of robbery, the person must (1) commit larceny (2) by force, threat of force, or intimidation. In contrast, to convict a person of conspiracy to commit robbery, the person must agree with another to commit a robbery. The conspiracy *is distinct from the criminal act itself*. Accordingly, robbery is not an element of the offense of conspiracy to commit robbery, and thus each crime has an element not in the other. Accordingly, these are distinct offenses as understood by the Double Jeopardy Clause. Therefore, John's double jeopardy defense will not succeed.

<u>Call C</u>

John should appeal to the Court of Appeals of Virginia. The Court has jurisdiction over criminal appeals from a circuit court, among other areas.

Conclusion

Introduction

By now, you should have a reasonably good understanding of how to write an effective essay on the bar exam. If you completed this book before starting your comprehensive review, as we recommended, you should have a leg up on your fellow test takers. Now is the time to work hard to learn the rules and their intricacies. As you do this, you will have an opportunity to revisit the techniques described in this book and to gain even further practice writing.

Much like the lessons Mr. Miyagi presented to his student in *The Karate Kid*, the exercises we presented to you in this book were intended to subtly teach certain lessons through repetition. In that vein, here are some simple lessons to remember for exam day.

Lessons to Remember for Test Day

Plan and Outline Your Answer Before Writing

You should plan and outline your essay before writing it. Do not spend too long doing this, but do not avoid it. If you spend a mere five to ten minutes doing this, your answer will most likely be reasonably organized. In fact, a good outline should allow you to state your conclusion up front. You do not need to necessarily write out an outline for every question, but for the complex questions, a written outline may prove especially invaluable. As you organize your answer, simply remember the steps detailed in this book. Consider the true issue the question is driving at. Recall the rule associated with that issue, and then associate facts in the question with the rule. Consider what you will say in the analysis and draw a conclusion. Then begin by writing that conclusion, including a "because" clause, if possible, to point the grader to the issue presented by the question.

Identify Issues That Generate Analysis

Remember, the bar examiners are testing issues that generate a fair amount of analysis. Of course, some questions may have multiple calls, some of which are very straight forward procedural questions, e.g., "What court should you file your action in?" However, every essay question will have one major call that asks you for significant analysis, e.g., "Is the defendant liable for negligence?" If you find yourself thinking or writing very little on these sorts of calls, think again. Somewhere the examiners have given you a rich issue with a little back and forth. You need to find it.

Skip a Tough Question and Return To It Later

If you quickly skim through the questions before the start of the test, you will most likely find some questions that seem much more difficult than others. Nevertheless, do the questions in order if you can, as this will ensure that you do not cause any confusion by answering questions in some haphazard order. As you tackle each question, ask yourself early whether you will be able to answer the question with enough time left over for the others. If you believe that the question is going to take too much time, skip it, especially if you know that other questions follow after it that are much easier to answer. Then, return to the unanswered question and do the best you can with the time remaining.

Have Faith in Your Abilities

Look at the bar exam question and tell yourself you know the answer. Chances are you probably do. Remember, by the time you sit down to the exam, you have spent upwards of three months studying for this exam. You have no doubt practiced many MBE questions and written essays. If you have mastered the method and style presented by this book, you will have a leg up on the other test takers. While others may write with little direction and employ bad syntax and grammar, you will have a thought-out, well-crafted essay. Be confident.

Page 85

Pace Yourself

When you begin writing, you may find yourself daunted with the task. Do not be. Now is your time to shine. Take your time and think things through carefully. However, do not take too much time on any particular question. Remember to write efficiently by saying only what you need to say to get to an answer to the particular question. If you talk about superfluous issues, you may find yourself with less time to dedicate to primary issues on other essay questions.

Final Thoughts

You have come far in your journey. Take stock of all the hard work you have done. If test day is tomorrow or soon, remember to rest well. On the day before the test relax and unwind. Do not study. It will not be long before you get to call yourself "attorney."

Good luck!

About the Authors

Andrew P. Connors is a Virginia attorney currently working as a judicial law clerk. He received his J.D. from Liberty University School of Law and his B.S. in Applied Mathematics from the University of Virginia. He was a Managing Editor of the Liberty University Law Review and an accomplished moot court competitor. He was the 4th Best Advocate in the Washington, D.C. region of the 2010 American Bar Association National Appellate Advocacy Competition, among other accomplishments. He enjoys reading, writing, and spending time with his wonderful wife, Allison.

Cherie Washburn is a practicing Virginia attorney. She received her J.D. from Liberty University School of Law and her bachelor's degree from Old Dominion University. In law school she won the Washington, D.C. regional competition of the 2009 American Bar Association Negotiation Competition. She is married and lives with her husband and loyal Great Dane, Molly. She enjoys running, skiing and beach vacations. She mentors in her spare time and volunteers in her community with the elderly.

Esquire Education

Making Better Lawyers

Get the help you need to succeed!

Get free tips and advice at our website, and learn more about our workshops and personalized instruction.

http://esqeducation.com

Made in the USA
Middletown, DE
23 June 2016